THE GEARHEAD'S GUIDE TO STOCK CARS

BY LISA J. AMSTUTZ

CAPSTONE PRESS
a capstone imprint

Published by Spark, an imprint of Capstone
1710 Roe Crest Drive, North Mankato, Minnesota 56003
capstonepub.com

Copyright © 2023 by Capstone. All rights reserved. No part of this publication may be reproduced in whole or in part, or stored in a retrieval system, or transmitted in any form or by any means, electronic, mechanical, photocopying, recording, or otherwise, without written permission of the publisher.

Library of Congress Cataloging-in-Publication Data is available on the Library of Congress website.
ISBN: 9781666356496 (hardcover)
ISBN: 9781666356502 (ebook PDF)

Summary: Stock cars zoom around race tracks with power and speed. But these vehicles can be made even faster and cooler, and readers will love finding out how. This high-interest book's accessible text and dynamic photographs put readers in the driver's seat.

Editorial Credits
Editor: Erika L. Shores; Designer: Heidi Thompson; Media Researchers: Jo Miller and Pam Mitsakos; Production Specialist: Tori Abraham

Image Credits
Getty Images: avid_creative, Cover, Icon Sportswire, 7, 23; Shutterstock: Bruce Alan Bennett, 17, 25, 27, 29; Shutterstock: Drew300, 13, Fabio Pagani, 8, 26, Grindstone Media Group, 5, 11, 15, 18, 21, 25, 28, i3alda, throughout, design element, Richard Thornton, 9, Sista Vongjintanaruks, 19

All internet sites appearing in back matter were available and accurate when this book was sent to press.

Capstone thanks Kevin Dick, technology education instructor in Mankato, MN, for his assistance in reviewing this book.

Printed in the United States   6413

Table of Contents

READY TO RACE 4
START YOUR ENGINES 6
STRONG AS STEEL 14
LOOKING GOOD 24
    GLOSSARY 30
    READ MORE 31
    INTERNET SITES 31
    INDEX 32
    ABOUT THE AUTHOR 32

Words in **bold** are in the glossary.

Ready to Race

Stock cars whiz around the track. They reach high speeds. Stock cars look like regular cars. But they are not the same inside. They are **modified** for speed.

NASCAR sets rules for stock car racing. There are other racing groups too. They have their own racing rules.

FACT
NASCAR stands for National Association for Stock Car Auto Racing.

Start Your Engines

Many stock cars have V8 engines. NASCAR has rules on engines. Cars are checked before and after each race. The engines can have up to 670 **horsepower**. At some tracks, horsepower is limited to 450.

FACT
Some stock cars can go 0 to 60 miles per hour in 3 seconds.

Stock cars need slicks for paved tracks. These smooth tires have no **tread**. They are wider and softer than regular car tires. This helps them grip the track.

The tires have an inner liner. If the outer tire goes flat, the inner one stays inflated. It helps prevent crashes.

It gets very hot inside a stock car. The cars don't have air conditioning. A back blower is often added. It cools a driver's legs and back. Fresh air blows through the driver's helmet too.

Stock cars with **manual transmissions** give the driver more control. Drivers shift gears when they speed up or slow down. Transmissions take a beating. Parts are often replaced after every race.

FACT
NASCAR races are 200 to 600 miles long.

Strong as Steel

A stock car spins out of control. It hits the wall. Bang!

Stock cars crash—a lot. The car's frame must be strong. NASCAR frames are made of thick steel tubes.

Stock cars are often longer and wider than street cars. They don't have doors. The driver climbs in through the window. Doors could fly open or get crushed in a crash.

FACT
Stock cars have only one seat. This helps make the car lighter and faster.

Stock cars must stand up to extreme speed and heat. Parts are made by hand. NASCAR parts must follow a **template**. Roll cages are added to stock cars. They keep drivers safe in a crash.

Race cars make tight turns. Spoilers on the back come in handy. They change the airflow around the car. This keeps air from lifting the car. It keeps the car from tipping over too.

Windshields on NASCAR cars are made of Lexan. This **material** is strong but soft. It will not shatter if something hits it. A clear film is put over the windshield for the race. It keeps the windshield from getting scratched.

FACT
Stock cars that race on dirt tracks have wire mesh screens instead of windshields.

Looking Good

Stock car drivers wear fireproof suits. They protect drivers in crashes. But the suits look cool too. They come in many colors and patterns. Drivers often add team patches.

Each stock car has its own look. Many are painted with bright colors. NASCAR cars aren't painted. They're wrapped in **viny**l. Vinyl wraps are easy to change. Details can be added too.

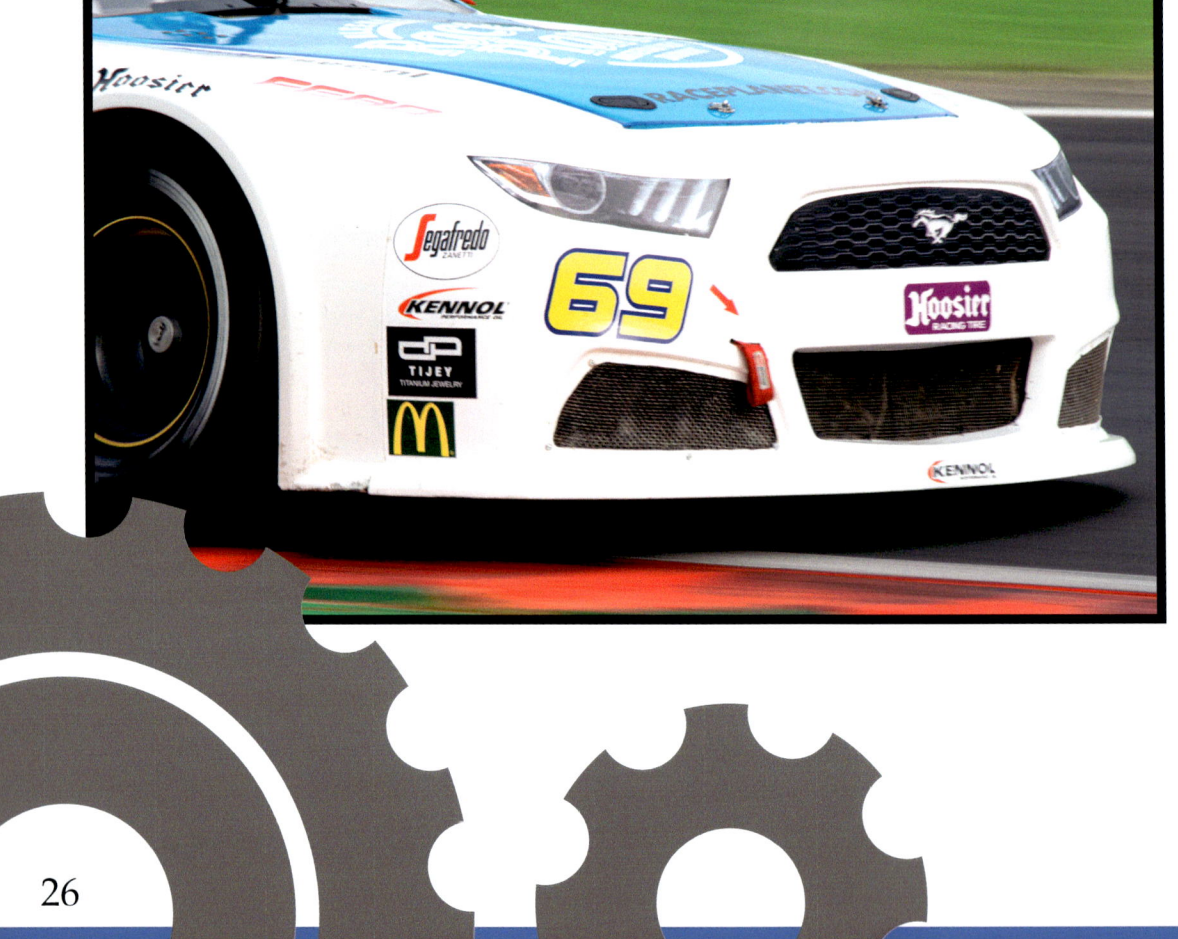

Cars flash past the finish line. The checkered flag waves. The race is over.

The crew checks the car. They fix any damage. They put on new tires. Next time, their stock car will be the fastest on the track!

Glossary

horsepower (HORS-pou-ur)—a unit for measuring an engine's power

manual transmission (MAN-yoo-uhl trans-MISH-uhn)—the series of gears that send power from the engine to the wheels

material (muh-TIHR-ee-uhl)—what something is made of

modified (MOD-uh-fyd)—changed for a specific purpose

template (TEM-plate)—a pattern that is followed as an example for how to make something

tread (TRED)—the pattern of raised lines on a tire

vinyl (VYE-nuhl)—a soft, shiny plastic

Read More

Doeden, Matt. *Stock Cars*. North Mankato, MN: Capstone Press, 2019.

Fishman, Jon M. *Cool Stock Cars*. Minneapolis: Lerner Publications, 2019.

Huddleston, Emma. *Stock Cars*. Minnetonka, MN: Kaleidoscope Pub. Inc., 2019.

Internet Sites

Auto Racing Facts for Kids
kids.kiddle.co/Auto_racing#Stock_car_racing

My First NASCAR Race
sikids.com/kid-reporter/my-first-nascar-race

Race Cars
dkfindout.com/us/transportation/history-cars/race-cars/

Index

back blowers, 10

crashes, 8, 14, 16, 18, 24

doors, 16

engines, 6

frames, 14

helmets, 10

horsepower, 6

NASCAR, 4, 6, 12, 14, 18, 22, 26

roll cages, 18

rules, 4, 6

seats, 16

slicks, 8

spoilers, 20

suits, 24

templates, 18

tires, 8, 29

transmissions, 12

vinyl wraps, 26

windshields, 22

About the Author

Lisa J. Amstutz is the author of more than 150 books for children. She enjoys reading and writing about science and technology. Lisa lives on a small farm in Ohio with her family.